PRAIRIE DESIGNS II
FOR STAINED GLASS WINDOWS

PUBLISHED BY:

CLIFFSIDE STUDIO
PO BOX 343
Marshalls Creek, PA 18335-0343 USA

ISBN 0-9641597-5-9

48 ORIGINAL DESIGNS
BY ALEX SPATZ

INTRODUCTION

To those of you who may not be familiar with my previous books, this book follows **Prairie Designs for Stained Glass Windows.** The work in these books are original designs in the Prairie School of Design which was developed by Frank Lloyd Wright.

Wright developed his Prairie School of Design from living in the midwestern prairie and learning to appreciate nature. His philosophy for his designs was: simplicity, unity and nature. Wright designed all of the aspects of his buildings including furniture, accessories and stained glass windows. In designing windows, he felt that they should be designed with straight lines to reflect the qualities of the metal and glass components in the buildings. He also looked to nature for his themes incorporating plants, flowers and their colors into his stained glass windows.

The purpose of this book is to give stained glass enthusiasts the opportunity to use the beauty of this simple yet elegant style of design in their own stained glass windows. It is a book for those who are beyond the basics in stained glass, that is why there are no "how to" instructions in this book.

I sincerely hope that everyone who uses the designs in this book will enjoy the simplicity and beauty of the Prairie School of design as much as I do.

WINDOW CONSTRUCTION

The windows in Frank Lloyd Wrights buildings were constructed with zinc came. This gave them added strength and gave Wright freedom to design without worry of structural weakness. I don't feel that it is necessary to make the designs in this book with zinc came. If you would like to try using zinc came, this would be a good opportunity, however, copper foil or lead came will also do fine. I do urge you to use rebar or copper foil reinforcement in appropriate places in the designs and especially in the free-form hanging designs.

COLOR

Choosing glass colors is a matter of personal choice, however, I would like to make some general suggestions. Wright used colors that he found in nature: yellows, ambers, greens, browns, reds and off-white. He also used mostly clear glass for the background of his windows. Some substitues for clear glass could be textured clear glass or light colored cathedrals. The smaller squares, rectangles and triangles of the designs are generally where you would want to use the stronger colors mentioned above.

ENLARGEMENT

The designs in this book are drawn to the scale of 1" = 6" (You can measure the drawings with a pica ruler.) This means that a design measuring 5" x 6" would be 30" x 36" full size. It is possible to measure and draw the designs by hand. Most of the spaces are in inch increments and the angles are mostly 30°, 45° and 60°. Of course, using a projector is a reliable method, also.

Cross

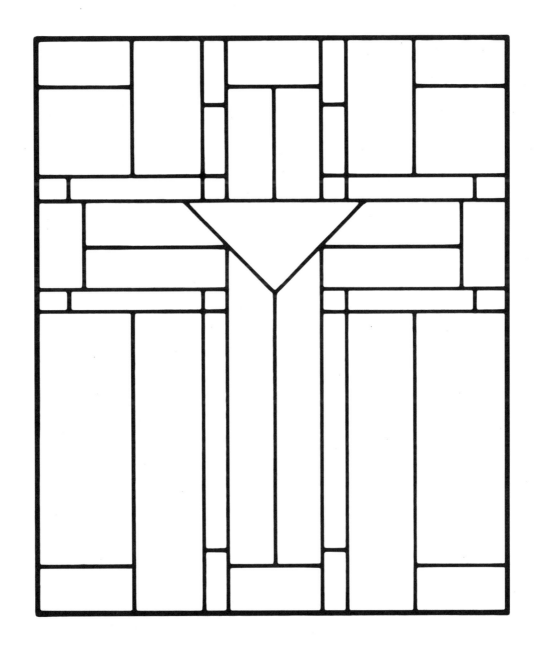

Diamond

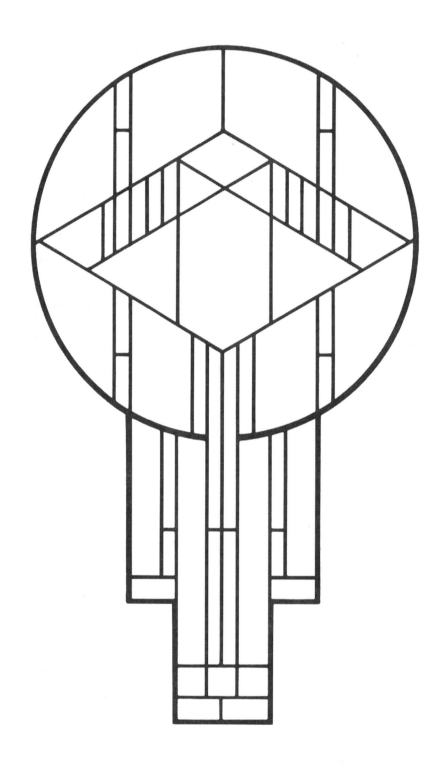

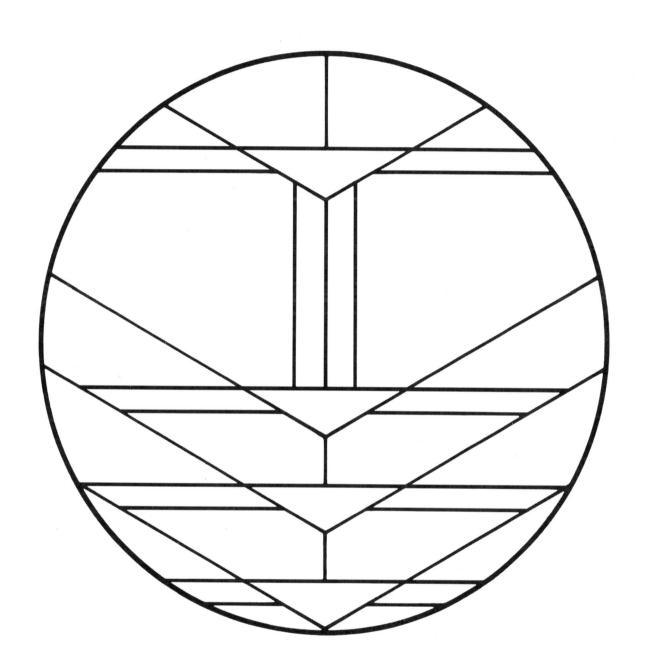

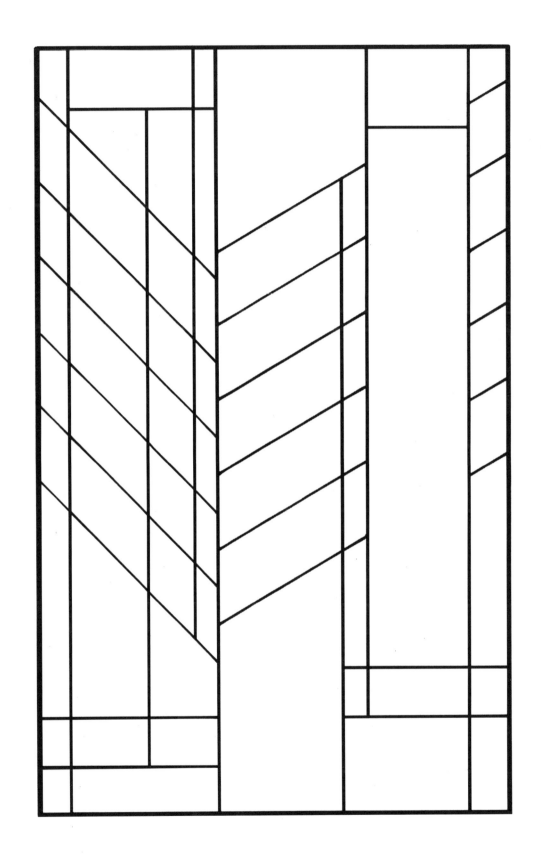

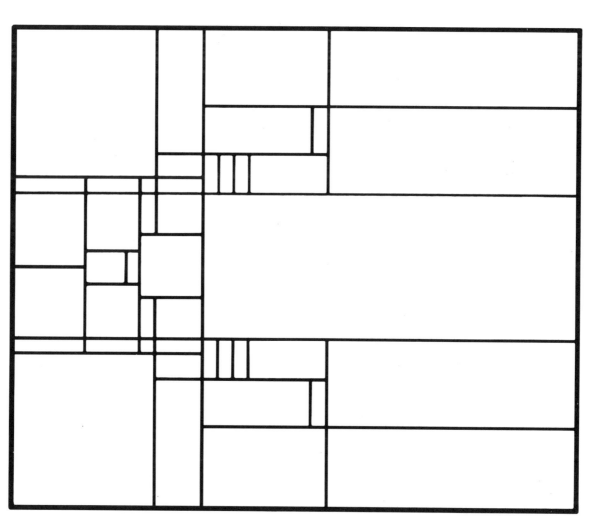

Bottom

5

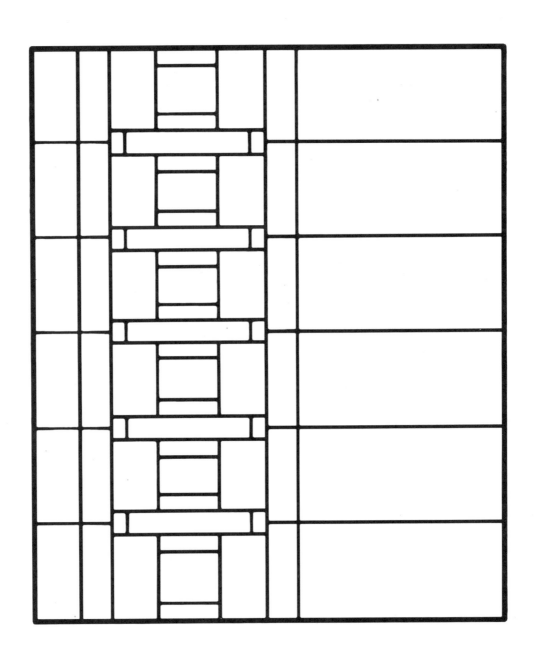

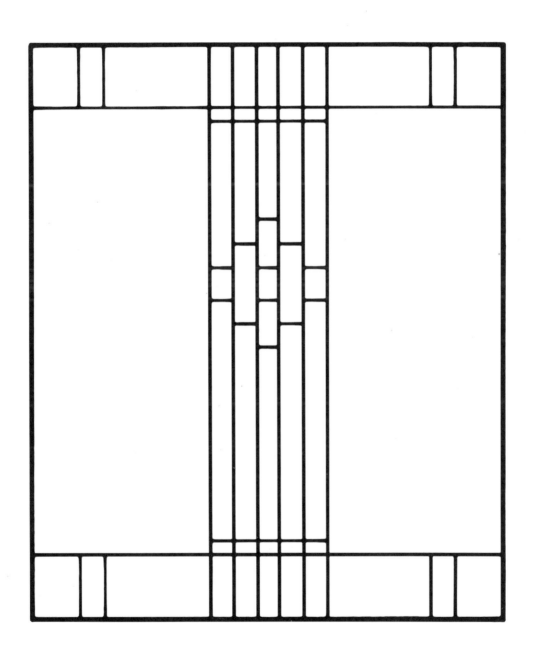

Butterfly

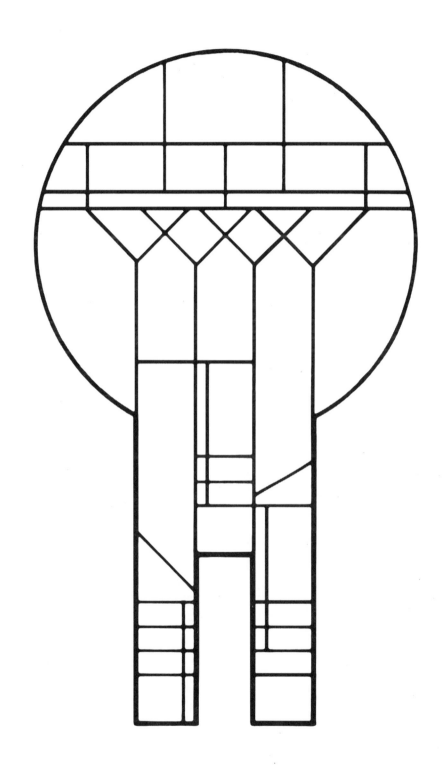

Triple Triangle Circle

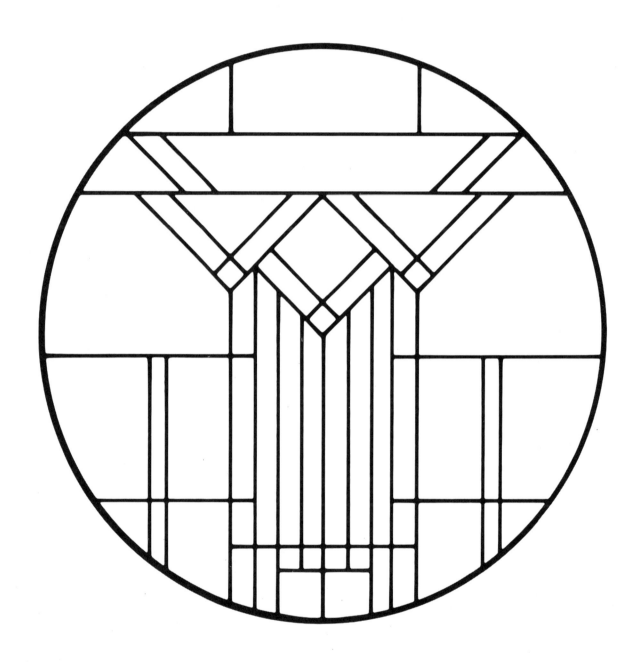

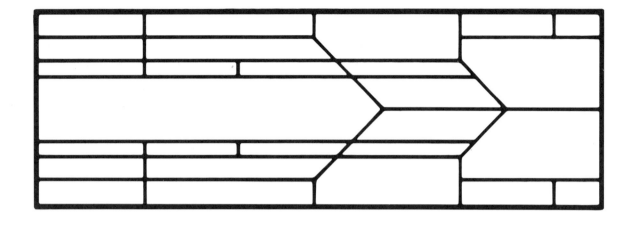

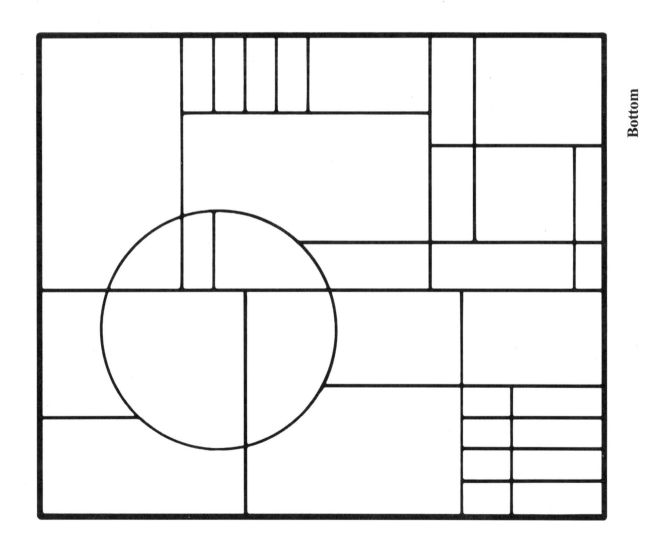

Crystalize

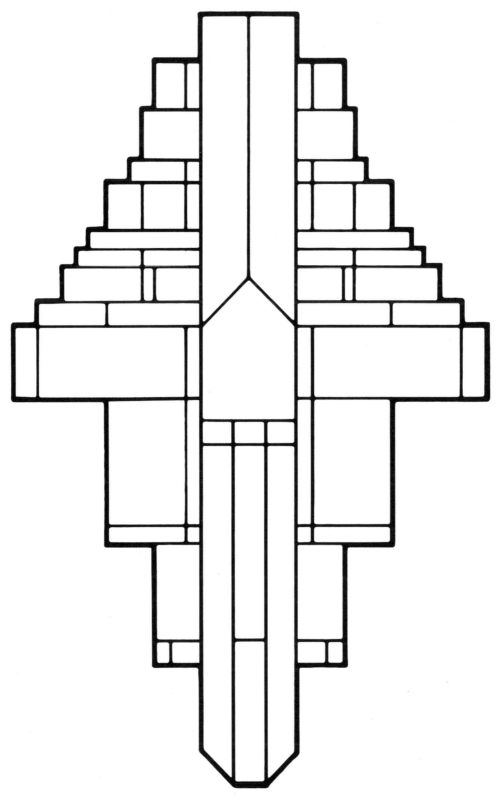

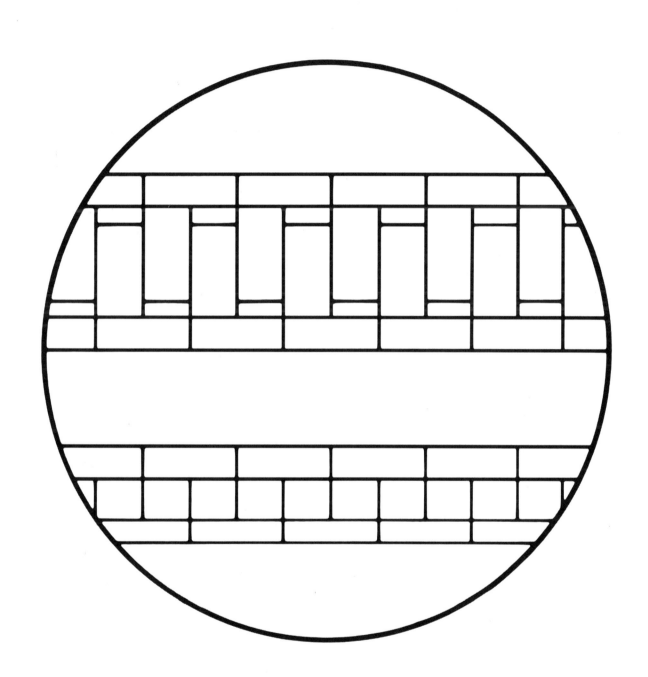

Rose

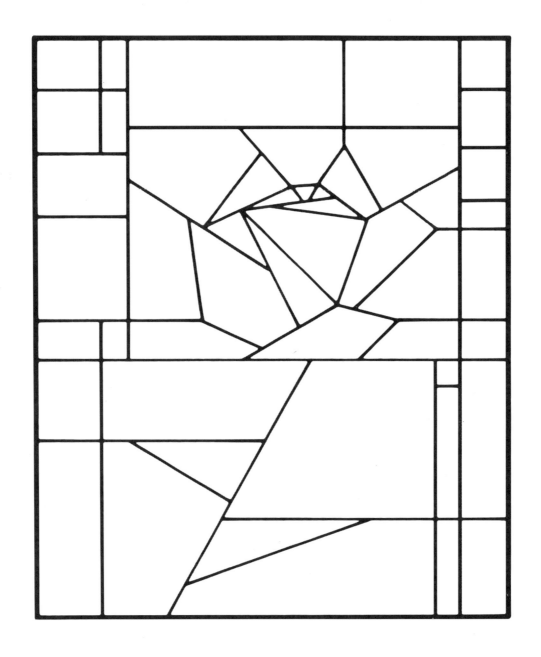

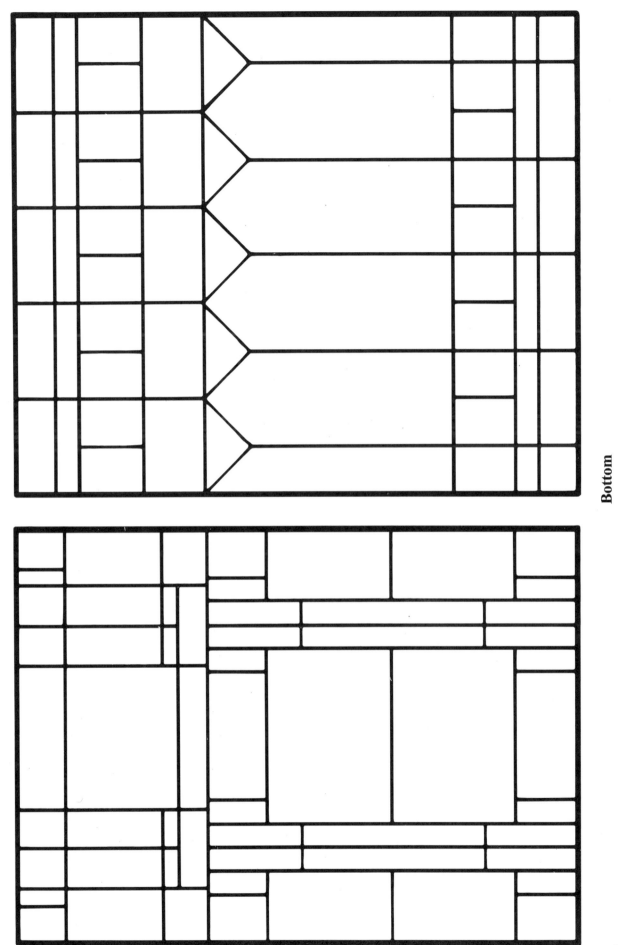

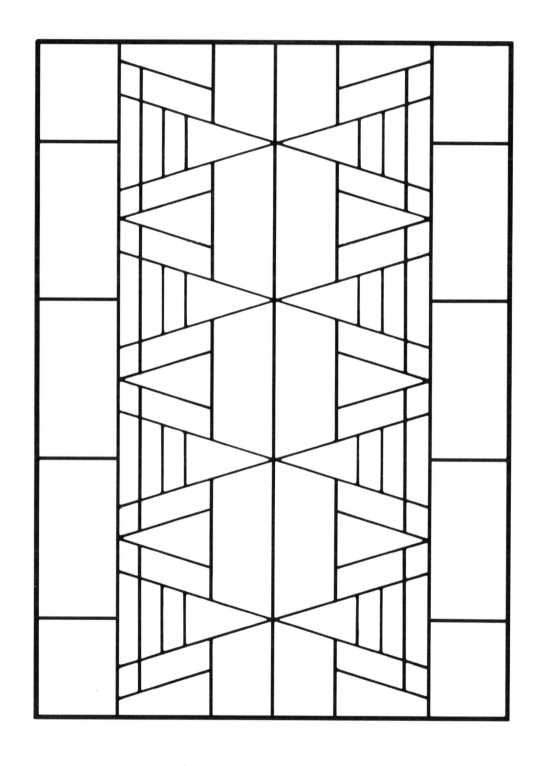

16

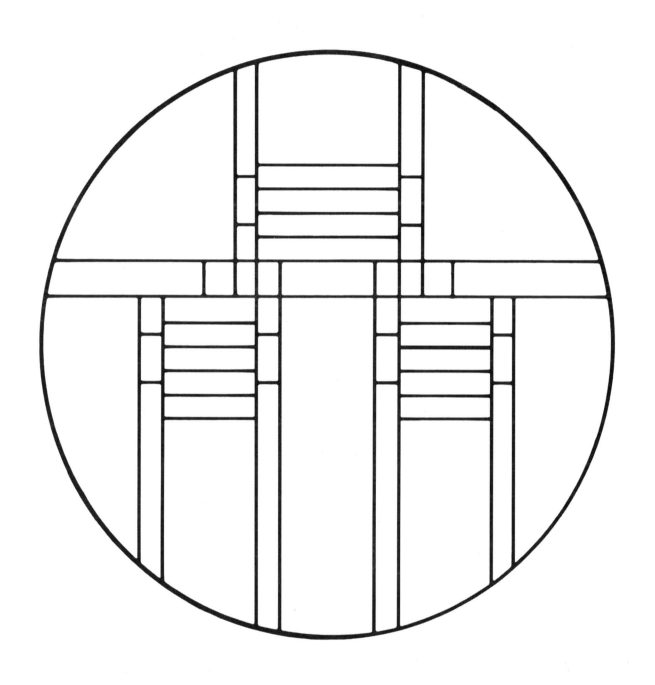

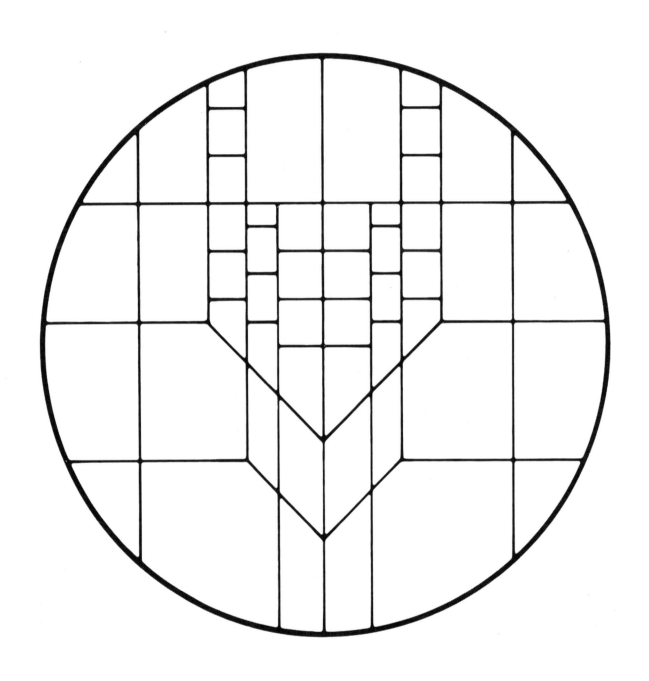

Millennium

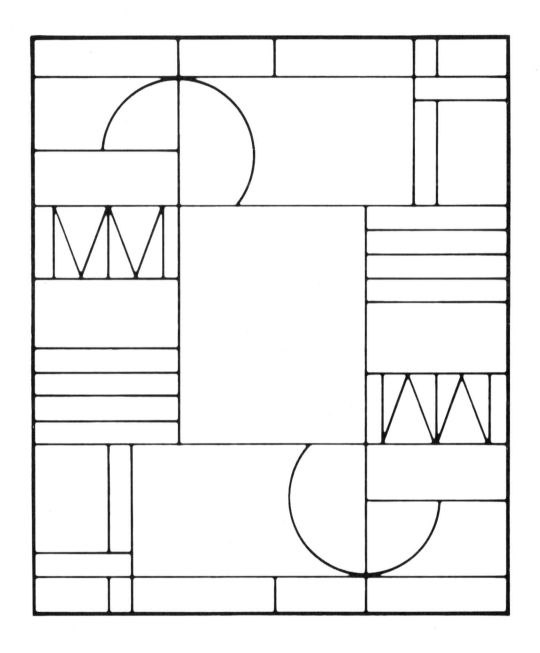

Sundown

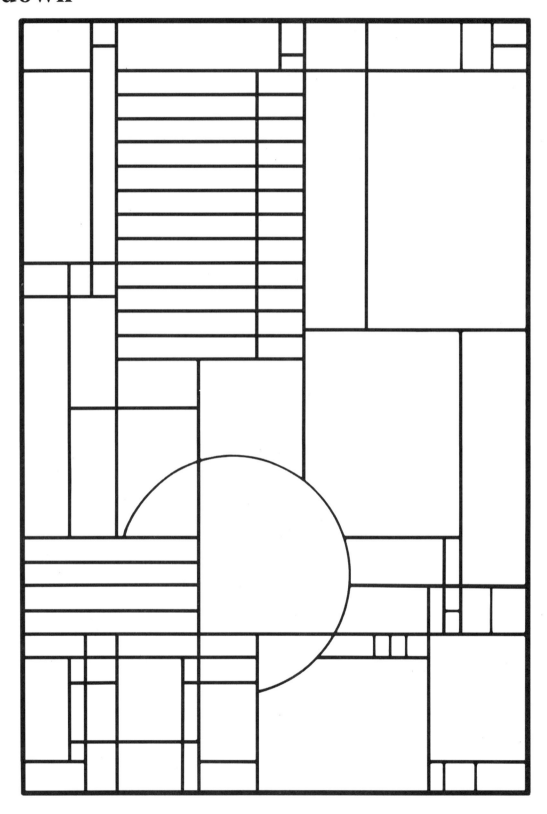

20

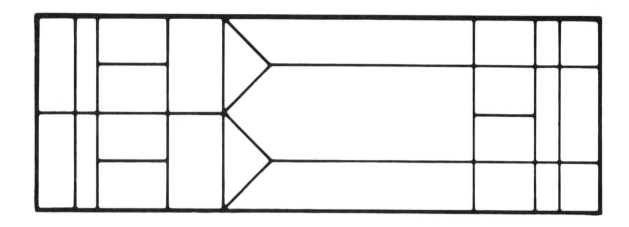

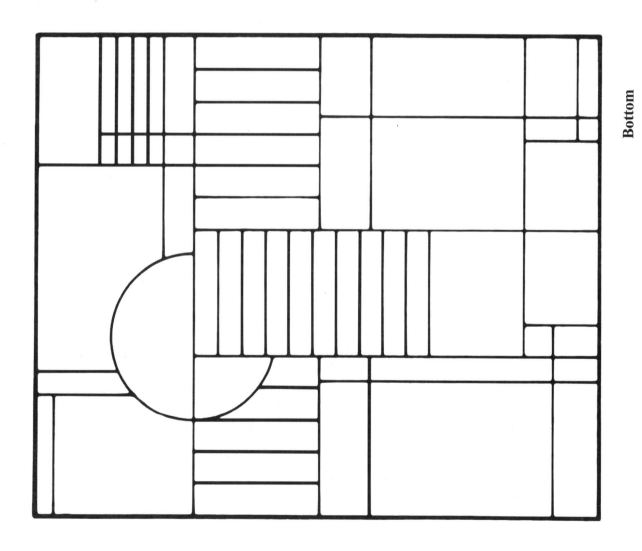

Irises

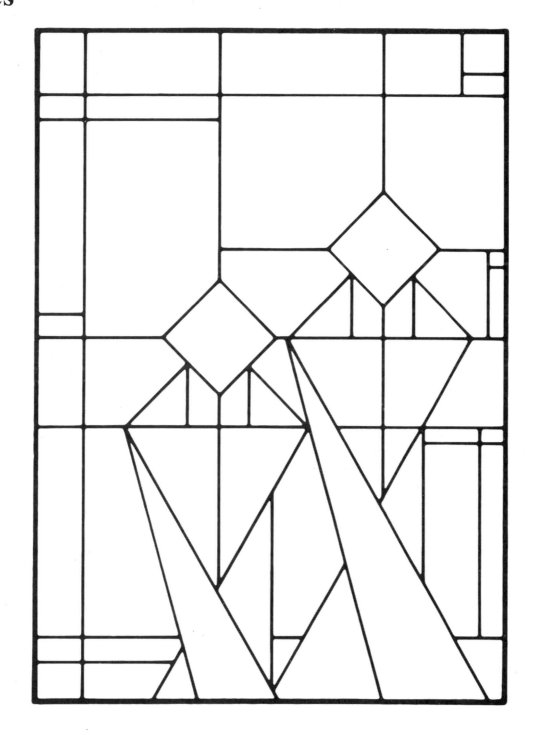

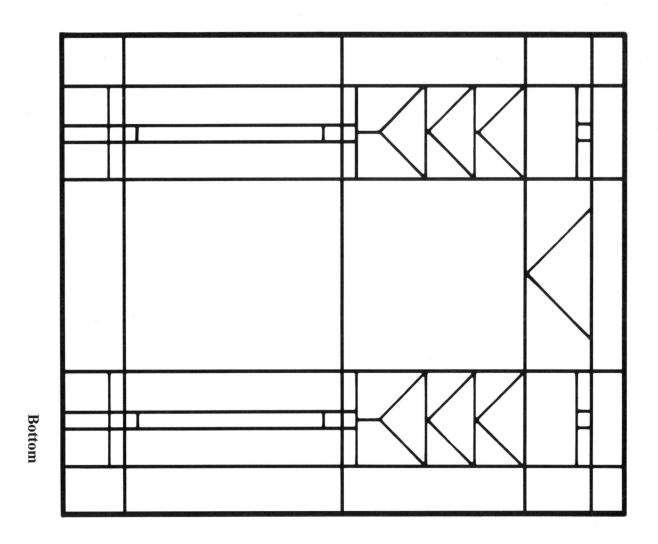

Bottom

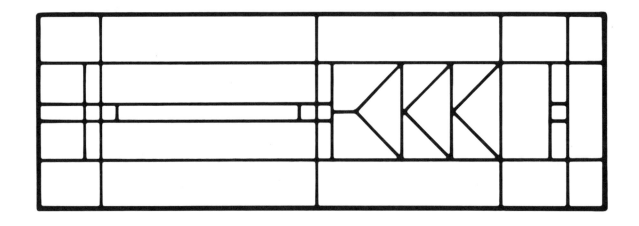

Four Corners

Sunbeams

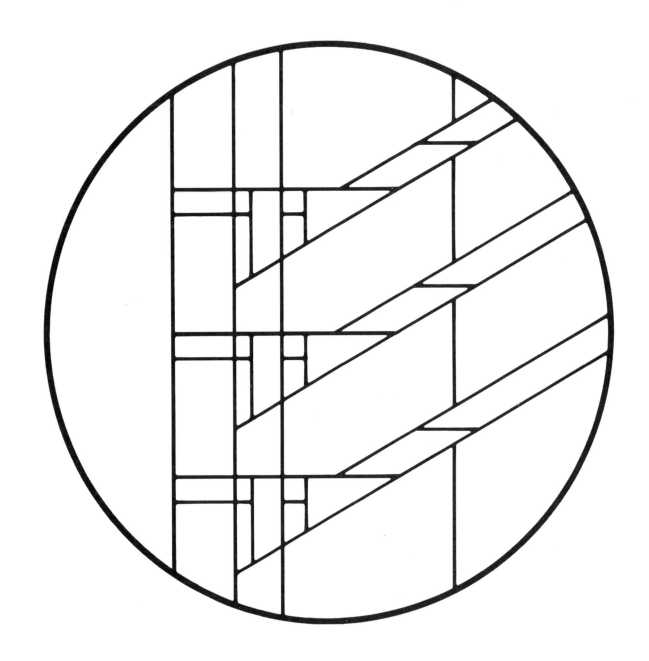

Desert Flower

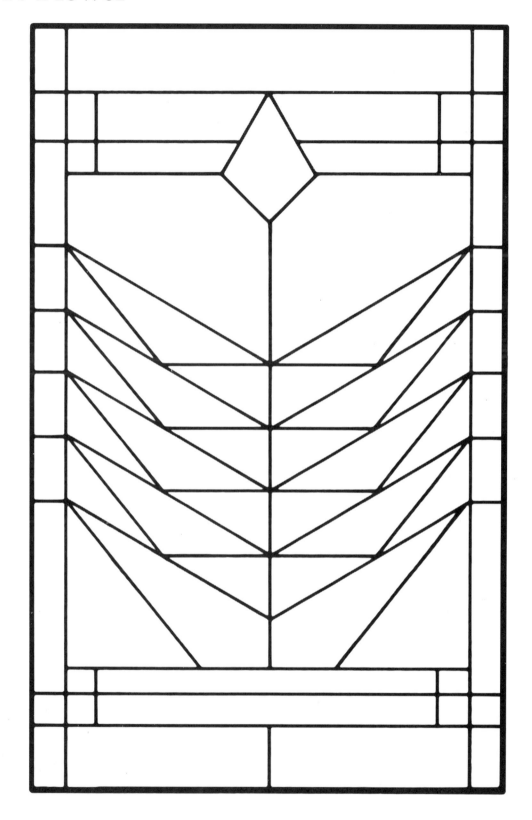

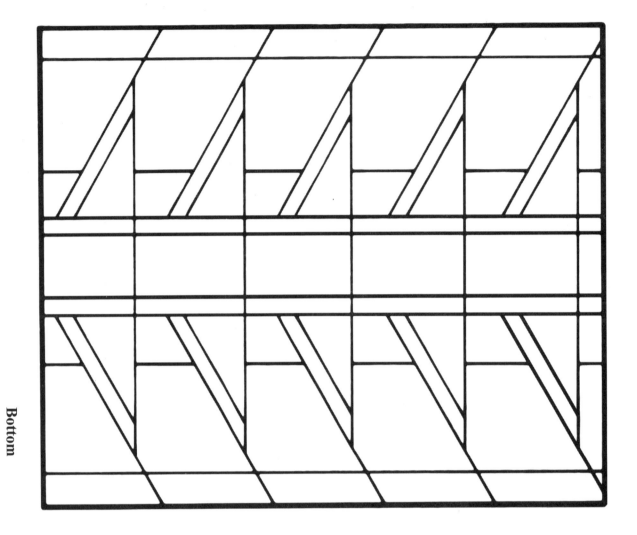

Bottom

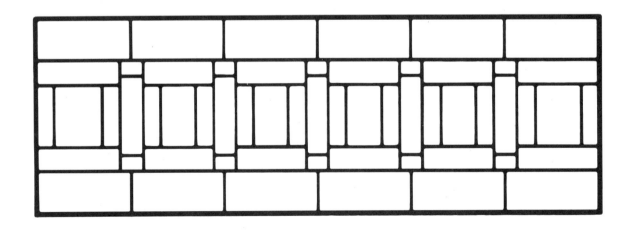

28

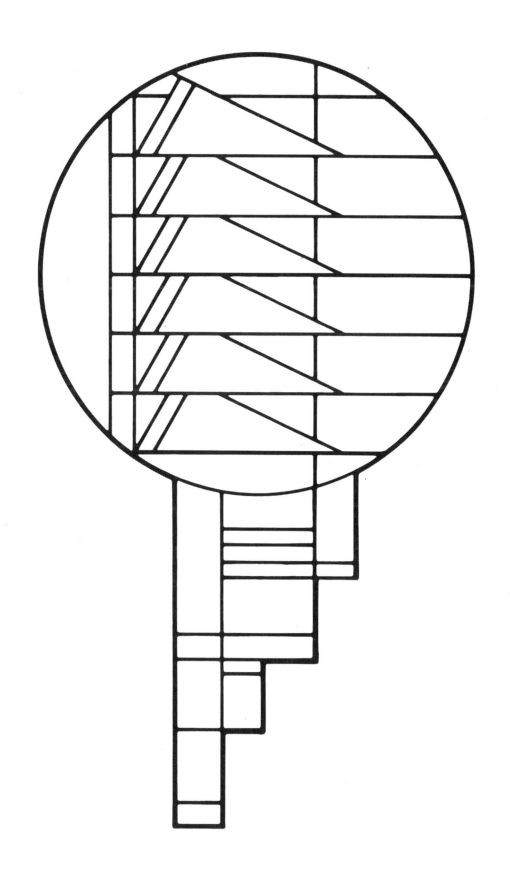

Reflection

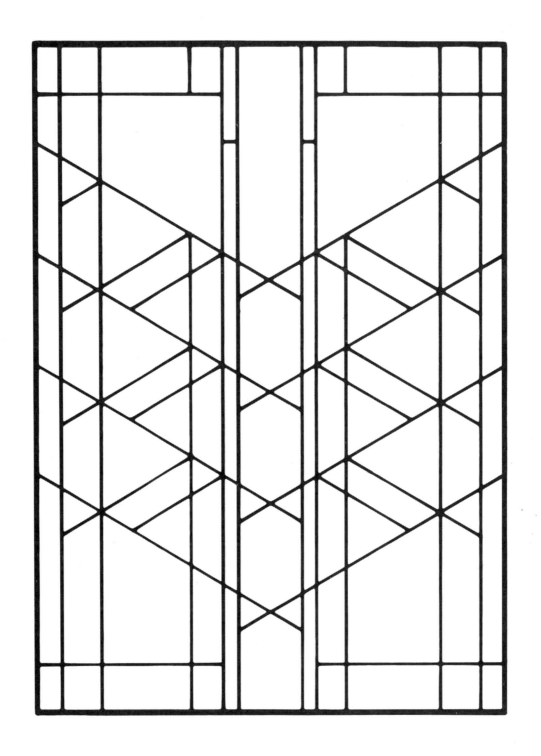

Intersection

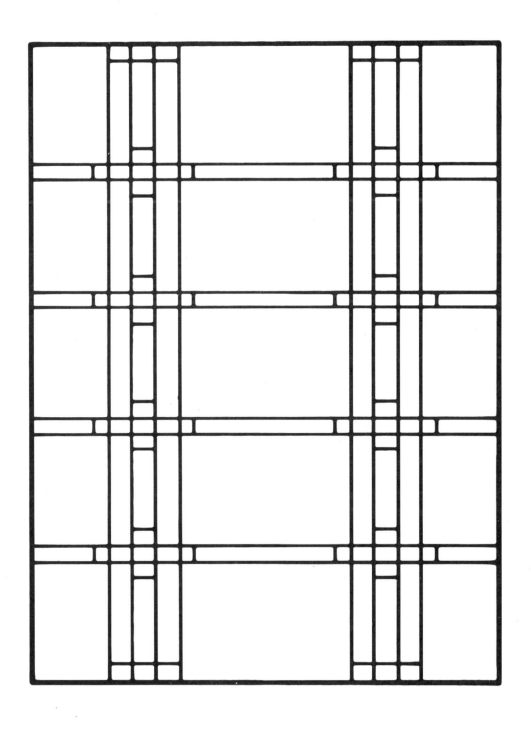

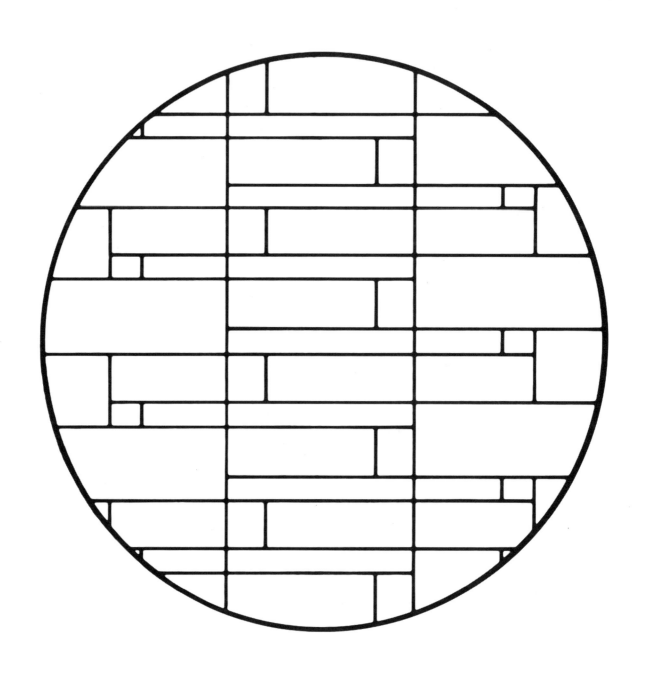

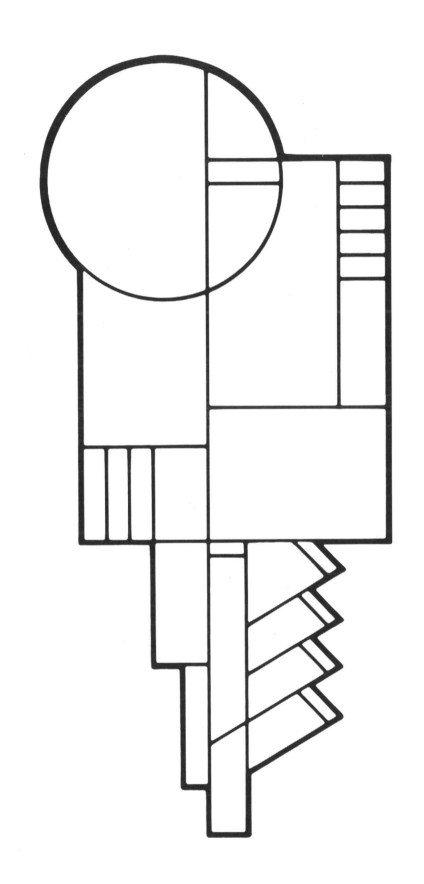

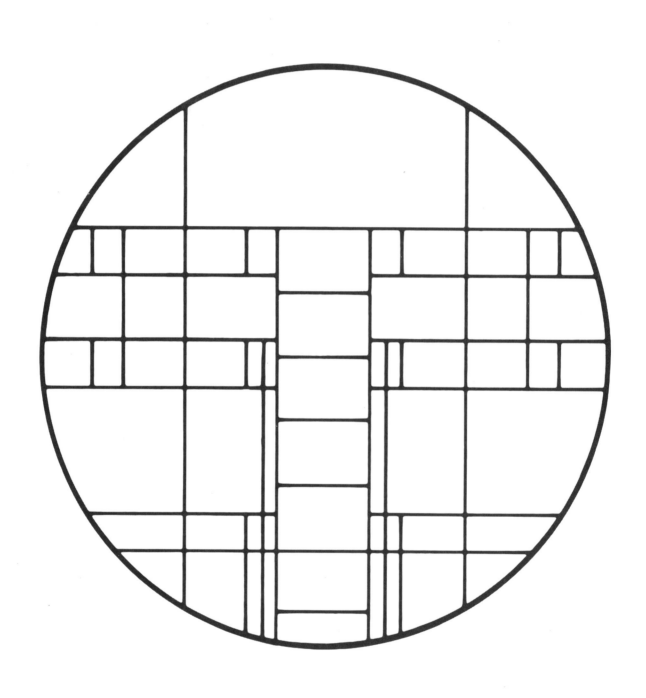

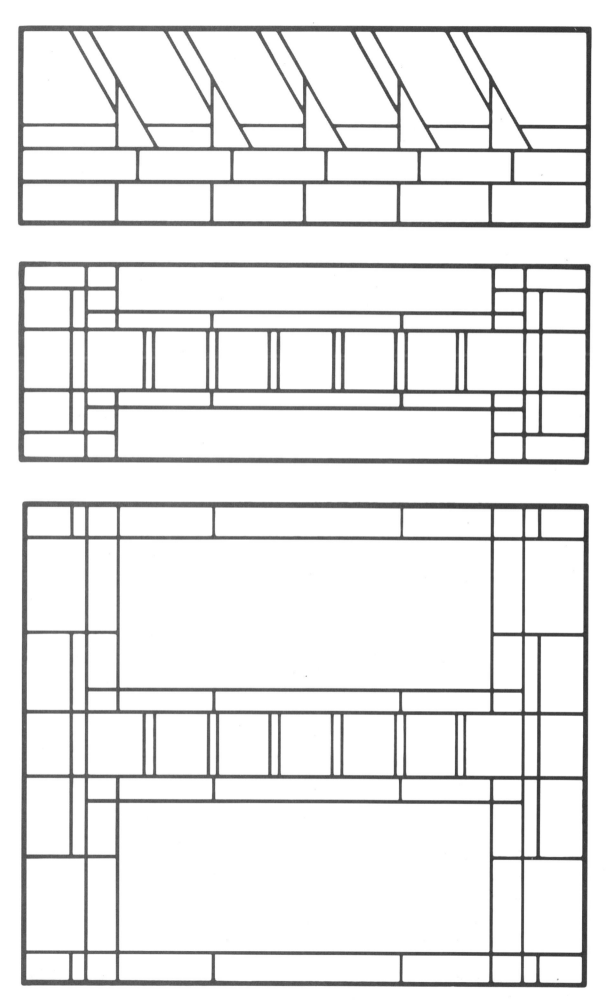

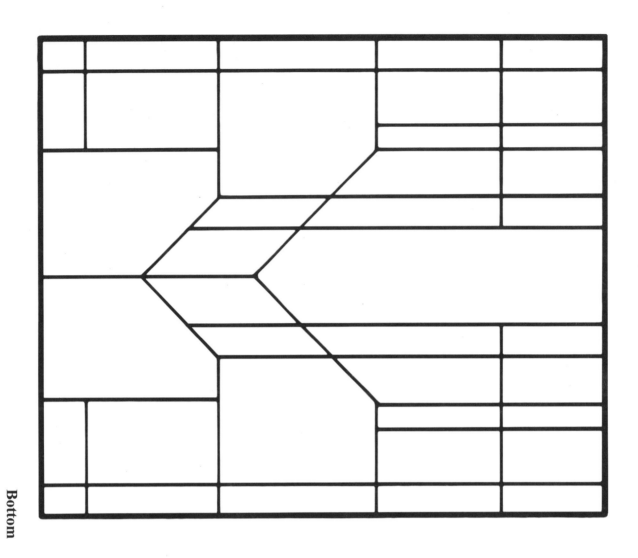

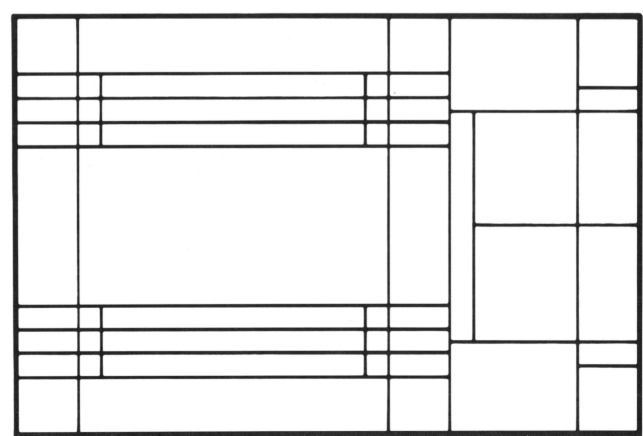

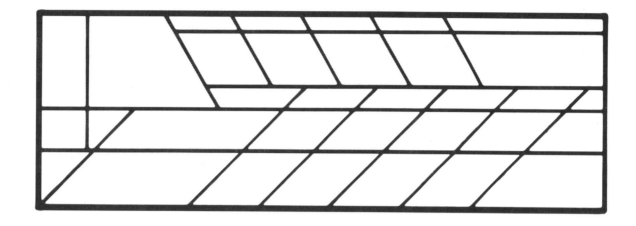

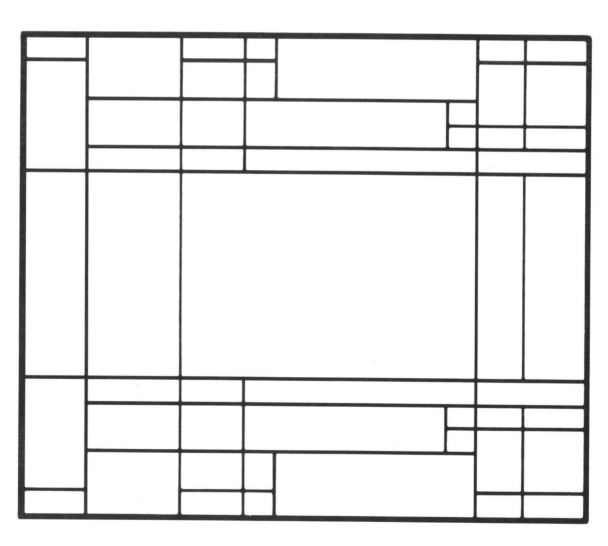

Bottom

37

38